Sam Sampson
Halcyon Ghosts

AUCKLAND
UNIVERSITY
PRESS

First published 2014

Auckland University Press
University of Auckland
Private Bag 92019
Auckland 1142
New Zealand
www.press.auckland.ac.nz

ISBN 978 1 86940 816 9

A catalogue record for this book is available from the National Library of New Zealand

Author photograph: Josh Hetherington

Cover image: decomposed nitrate film clipping from the Turconi Collection, Moving Image
Department, George Eastman House, International Museum of Photography and Film
Cover design: Jacinda Torrance, Verso Visual

Printed by 1010 Printing International Ltd

Halcyon Ghosts

Contents

for Doris May Scotting

*Hand in hand with equal plod they go. In the free hands — no.
Free empty hands. Backs turned both bowed with equal plod they
go. The child hand raised to reach the holding hand. Hold the old
holding hand. Hold and be held. Plod on and never recede. Slowly
with never a pause plod on and never recede. Backs turned. Both
bowed. Joined by held holding hands. Plod on as one. One shade.
Another shade.* — SAMUEL BECKETT

& Lucia Torrance Sampson

The Kid

Watch Charlie Chaplin un-
wind
    listen in-
tently to that blind
   mazy course
      running wild

through all forms of mim-
   icry, fun-making and clog-dancing

    childhood imbroglio

old-school sheet music

   where landscapes are raised
    used stamps stick

   a trio for three bassoons

    a lane of horse-chesnut trees

   a red bus   turns
this city past, passing … the Queen's Head

    the horse-drawn bakery van
  the booby hatch
    … framed fixtures
streams from some old world mix …

   tinker, tailor, soldier, sailor …

....

where pigs roamed
        a mill :
    villagers   peasants, villains
three craftsmen   two slaves, one tramp

    the total number housed
in a small brick building
    rebuilt twice
built from playground to dalliance ...

    rich man, poor man, beggar-man, thief ...

....

    Doris May ... re-
  visit this institution   :
          1931

a school for the orphaned and destitute children

modern times .... rest-
    oration ... O on song *we'll-*
  get along   :

      (in time)

    as body   *shadow*
  and light   *... reel*

a-shrug-and-a-kick

come-shadow-shadow-come
and cut . . .

(on film)

mirror images . . .

over-
lapping scraps . . .

the evanescent

smile　　　*(likeness)*　　　*chorus*

of that　　　*unknown*

. . . lady, baby, gypsy, queen.

in memory of my grandmother

… and I dreamed we were still alive
dreamed we were not yet born
dreamed we were yet to be.
— MICHAEL PALMER, *THREAD*

We are as free as birds. Only the birds aren't free.
We are as committed as birds and identically.
— JOHN CAGE

——————————————————ghosts

                    dress
                         as
                 mock
                    kings
                        s-
                        wear   dom
                            king-

                                        come

                                    door-
                            steps
                      sing-
                   songs
                of
              eco-
              logy
                hitch
            sun-
              sets
          to
            horizons
        dance
      ritual
chain-
        dances

halcyon————————————————————————

wear
    colour-
        ed
           em-
              broid-   waltz
                  eries   door-
           to-door
      leave
     colanders
on

                                        cemeteries
                                    local
                                  at
                                wires
                              on
                            settle
                    roads
                  cross-
                local
              at
            wires
          on
        settle

Ganges

&

the
          in
               priests
                    with
                              bathe

miracles
                                        &   masks
                              feather   wear
                    cloaks   -to-house
          perform   house
                                                  from
          winter   huia
                                        carry
                              luck
                         good
                    of
               wishes
          sing
     to
  gods
invite

&

ions

stat-

from

flew

flags

ed

colour-

bright

  lunar

                                                  cycles

                  thirteen
                              its
                            year
                              solar
                                      the
                                  it
                              round
                                  &
                                      sand
                                        amper-
                                                    &
                                          amp
                                            an

                                          chamber
                                              a
                                              &
                                        passage
                                            a
                                      both
                                earthed
                          land
                      Kings-
                  in
              placed
          jar
    a

sky &

the   the

across

degrees

thirteen

travels

moon

the

&

                                                    rangi
                                                  Titi-
                                                      in
                                                  &
                                                        structures
                                                            like
                                                      nest-
                                                          built
                                                      &
                                                        fishers
                                                      king-
                                                        to
                                                mice
                                                    fed
                                                  we
                                              day
                                          each
                                      &
                              &   fro
                          to
                      it
                    crossed
                star)
            dog-
              Dane
        ow   of Thor   Great)
    shad-

shaped

scones

buried

trees

tea-

round

a-

twine

of

types

different

tied

halcyon————————————————————

————

          marked
        the
    edge
         one
           of
   many
        circles …

                                                                                                            &

                  table
                   the
                    at
                XIII.............
                  left
                   &

              bread
          honey   (on orange)
        of
           &   green
     sacrifices   black
   offered   cheese   magenta
                  psalms
  shoes   swallowed
like

Erasure

history in a nearby tree
isolated sightings ~~(aligned by absence):~~ ~~huia extinct~~

for Don Binney, artist, conservationist

Doubled Lexicon

the horizon

     O

pens

the circle

     Sobin

circles the expanse   expands dirt

         distributes

     the liquescent

ellipse   :

     the glittering . . . . geometric design

of the glass-headed light

---

     two in-
complete oblong drops

     the pond of the Olive Tree

                    O
          pens
the mirror

          shadows swing the windrow

:

  ground

            rocky outcrops: composed of chalk and green sand
                              composed of shelly sandstone cliffs

          layers, over-
laying clays, marly macigno
                              the lignite field

_____

          erasure links the sentence

sentences the

pause

            recesses the sun

      O
                    pens

the corridor

(structure up-
    dates   a staircase disappears ...

                ceramic wind chimes
charred grape seeds
          Ionian soft paste
     pinkish circular bands)

  registers
as rectangular frames
    the utterance

awkward   doubled lexicon
  two diagonal lines

     at right angles
   the child centre   it-

self   dead-centre

   O

---

pens

the footnote

     calibrates ...
  passage

caresses   the eye-

lid-en————————————————
    closed circumference   deeply etched

          ligated   to the (be-
clouded)   presence of identical blocks
     printed in raw clay.

———————————————————————————————————

for Gustaf Sobin

Flushed from a Tidal Retreat

in the deep-freeze we
will feel no pain

just go to sleep (as if winter was coming)
it is 'asleep'

as in Rosei's dream
watermarked origami

from the fold   butter-
fly logic
                              to be : becalmed

afloat with the telling
sail said the lullaby

scissoring   and . . . captioned

...

elevation   ~~commotion and roseate histrionics~~

to see hills I didn't even know existed | rain transforming this patch |
spring eagles returning to the same nest | bodies – each in foetal position
| suicidal Inuit youth shackled hand-to-heart . . .

...

quieter moments when fights for food abate

… fog shrouds Snyder lake | a deer fords the main branch | riparian light
blinking on a dark field | the grotto where tradition states Jesus was
born,

        after descendants, not everyone believes : believes, fragrant
pastures celebrate love | jaguar dancers torment the mineral kingdom,
and the whorls (many coated) turn … El Niño churns in, disarming | the
last war is not over

…

        under the masked avatar
~~the body wills its incarnation~~

    … electrical improvisations

        ~~the young born miniature adjuncts~~

     (((collisions beneath the moon)))

  ghost moths generate night skirmishes

       wing-tips

~~shadowing the wall~~

      they balance at mechanical rest
a fold: one ghost upon

      another

       …

leverage in memory

          a rift between
   for instance   try
      to replace

~~(mise-en-scène)~~
      no need for excavations
   the process gifted

     grown in wild streams

FLUSHED FROM A TIDAL RETREAT
    RUSHED FROM A TIDAL RETREAT
     Shhh.

i.m. of my father, perched 40 years above Little Muddy Creek

All the Everlasting Cataracts

near at hand

rip-cords surround the centre

gurge of pulse

on / oft

to sometimes detect
actual remnants

to look up, and tell of this fractal shape

one gradual solitary star
which comes upon silence

...

fragments_____

that word startled up

filled in, in pencil
a transcript: the story dawned   outlines

nerveless, script-less, dead-

ends felt in every feature
eyes closed: bowed head listening to the earth

to an ever-revolving spiel

...

trace : tracer
one of two great circles
intersection: right angles at poles
nadir: the low
zenith   the high

circles and arcs
broad-belting colure

sages, keen-eyed astrologers
earth-bound evangelists

they study the sky
study the fault lines

(the god and sunrise)

both, and both in one
all along a dismal rack of clouds

upon the boundaries of day and night
a drifting mass

cloud
on
cloud

    the sky in-
       verse

       …

      nineteenth century

   slow-breathed melodies,
 like a rose in vermeil tint and shape

enter, but who entertains?
    effigies, visions, extras …

     opaline forms
  amorphous

  :   pictures of intimacy

 all the everlasting cataracts

     … pools

loops   these crystalline pavilions
  pure fields mantled by sea salt

…

re-cast the self-
same beat

in hollow shells

in the cadence of time
where a dead branch fell, there did it rest …

reset to follow, to turn and lead the way

a stream went voiceless by   (streamed)

mountainous: no shape extinguishable

when the bleak-gown pines
        when winter lifts his voice, a noise

the mysterious grate of wind in trees
        whether in calm or storm

(the same scene)

god of the sky : bookish séance

that old spirit-leaved book
sifted well … from the ion-universe

...

flames yield like mist

all calm through chaos and darkness
from chaos and darkness

the extraordinary

the constant … the inter-
nal law   and how
I

whether through conviction, or disdain
in this expressive line
quicken the patter of beads

(pearl beads drop-
ping from their string

ele-
mental nature
powerful similes

ponderous millstones)

…

appearance of strength
a deception masking real weakness

essence in its tent

before the winged thing

silver wings of dawn rising
now a silver line hints at this approach

in each face a glint of light
see how the light breaks in with this line

(haphazardly)

till suddenly a splendour
like morning

the horizon in noise

...

at the set of sun
light fades
first from the eastern sky

to one who travels from the dusking east
attributes of the wanderer

wondering in vain about
the inventor of god and music

of light and song

soft breaking noise

white melodious throat

a name signifies memory
would come as no mystery

pin-pricks of the world … name-sakes

for me variance
by knowledge only

the above and the below

gathering all things mortal
this endless commencing

this still,
steady light

brilliance
of the moon   O

independence
acknowledges no allegiance.

after John Keats's 'Hyperion'

I Spilled My Story

                  a raft plunged ...

picadored green people tethered to years wend their way, squawking about an adventure without a conch, conversation you could swim in, also magnify ...

        bubbles ... well-warped logicians ... ionised passages

    a deep-freeze refrigerates escapades and layers link the lake

        the ice harvest

    V-shaped bars   scene perched in Voice: loud hoo-hoooo ... bee, ze, ey, ay ... headlamps, holes in the skull   saw and lift off ... to enlarge we head upstairs over to the room full of holes ... sylvan slums

                O bright suit, white from place of the cruel rook, return
then be done
        (antiques draped in velvets)

    moth wired in the aquarium   (this scene is allowed)

voice ambushes and we are built to divine perseverance, orange amplified with cedar-beak : interior wall ... active aviary ... *bees breeze*

I have a number of poems

containing the known, the lowest, the hole in the middle.
I manage to stop myself like that. No not embarrassed. Finally
to stop. Rest. Turn on the lights ... the duration beneath tense
artifice: black : bulging, comprised of sea urchins (all which are
whiter if a bit starfish fades) ...

... exclusivity dwells in habitat

adaptable from desert to compass rose, the inherent nature of
construction. Cubist images: violins and guitars analogous to
costumes later designed as conforming to the soul ... there
are several areas of debate, the capacity of a single imagination:
emotion for analysis and the claims of a photographer detailing
colour with interest in the arc of a possible cause
(a likely cause which cannot leave a trace was omitted)

transparent blues, the trance of celestial parades ...

Eden, Lion, where beginnings grow easily, pleasing to the eye as to the general public, rest in these plants, the commonly grown cactus ... go west vagrant Tas wrote:

I can tell from here ... *what the inhabitants of Venus are like: they resemble the Moors, burned by the sun, full of wit and fire, always in love, writing verse, fond of music* ...

... and Deimos glows from afar (Pro webcam activated: Mars image: Phobos and Deimos, November 3)

I wait, resight it (usually offer the right choice)

head submerged 1-2-3 white eggs ring the river, numbers have the
capacity to sing thereby demonising forests … 4-5-6 at any time the
formation of ants sympathetic to the vibrational sounds of the poem,
alas howling engineers called for more and ships set sail across Kashmir
… wings, wailers and frescoes offset as trees, such a tongue, virtually
tongue lightning against the ceiling, clarification: conservation mainly
a tiny layer of soil, aeration critical of dots, the abundance of the Red Sea
and upon a smaller scale Atlantis, that bug-eyed canary, black-finned,
bluish-purple …

all year minute fish

stripes, silver below, Jan–June, Oct, above jets that are in fact outlines,
true bullet points dictating ancient records, momentarily plumes of
thought matched opposite beetles, days wed to cyclical support coupons:
an alternative happiness grazes rock bottom (like endless rock exhibited)
a reconnaissance, moving, tracking age …

the team applied a patina, running in the torturous wind (so long Rodin)
humans project the interior, seek definite articles : indefinite lamps, to
be used if only the moon healthy in the next world rises: an essence of
deceased peoples without any paraphernalia; we can only conclude that in
death, as in life … beads, flecks of the ice-tail …

... interned, burly bearded

Mr Zui a botanist-zoologist tasted it, arranging studies by radar and
radio telescopes … frequencies reset the sleep-O-matic … O how
it internalises voices … O how its presence sharks, and silver jacks
shutter: tiny fish guard historical reasons, and the worldly home spits
out simple configurations, like winging into the evening's fractured
yellow … languishing beneath the framed module; how it marked the
first stitches (like red sutures threading the Alaska Range) Anchorage
engaging from one end: unearthed, a salt-mine man sleeping as numerous
kings who had fallen on the fallowed year, the rare golden (sunset) with
its widespread digits: at the edge of town an anachronism: covered,
rediscovered plastic figurines …

Broken Architecture

If existence is structured
this colourful dust conquers and divides

                 its haughty composure
       elation; this heart aches

it was quite a rare thing to slide across grass
             bellicose, consider the earth

       to seize shadows I grab them by the sleeve
re-collection some lamp-like filament
     faces reawaken, rooted alone in a happy home
         neck turns, travelling to rejoin the spine

       every movement beneath the moon
squeaky space : displacement

         ...

       kind of mesmerising, a thoughtful yes
answer: *wait for me in the gardenias*

         hurry the list away, in no mood to barge in

           a face has been drowned, dragged below
      surely to utter no word, good or bad: stopped quite still

with a case history he knelt down
        eyes downcast, no sign of love and pleasantries
                a cheer that might have been smiling

      we heard a guitar strumming
           a guilty turn, thinking how cheerful
how respectful, how tangled, and how much loved by many

shall I go back and notate that thought?
      or may I stay and tell you about the (g) olden days

...

    nail her voice:
bone-flute, soft ... *kōauau*

          if music could surface
     listen: let a moist eye overflow

             so earnest and particular, rinse
    the bright light : drive the green fuse
strike out against whimsy

        how can we ever rest
   news calls the dead hour-after-hour
vistas trace famous expressions

       I remember the poet
  learning to turn his face from the anxious door
     symbols compact scent: *tantalising*

...

        no exchange, no ... not quite tongue yet
to hear your song, chance words spoken

       left in the alphabet soup
   only a week ago inked heaven
the owner shakes his head

       gives a shape to, hammers out compositions
          the character of this story is easily rendered
    (a mystery most profound)

     why waste tears or feign sorrow
worry, when skin must be glad
    she mutters, paces to and fro ... alone
     each branch will touch
       tell of

      what is to be done without disclosure
   reactions have not paid dividends
a cough freezing a moment

      hammered home in any direction ...
   nearly, and then falling back upon ground

...

a drawer opens through broken architecture
under breath we shall arrive at
                        the straight : stripped water course
            a whole configuration wired and attached

            difficulty in finding words to protest

(email transmits this attachment)

to dress, quit the slow boat's relief
            too kick and knock fails to get recognition

                        enter afterwards : remaindered
      in synchronicity the memorable interview
steel is voiceless, such a devil of a swipe

      apparatus our benefactor: I am tired, vocabulary deflated
                  broadcasts gave occasion to good-natured recollections

            sang of, and joked by,
then half-a-dozen turned and answered, very low:

      no one will ever whip the sea flat

            no one

                  ...

                  so very strangely, rejoin in a low act: label voice
      (scarcely audible) I will map, tell you, say by-the-way, open the book,
                  wait for a while ...

delay: wing bending down to bruise the child
believe me, I desire to see you safe

a little wild-life winter is hard to bear
pride sustains: had it been above board

we could watch the hilarious stitch reign

a box of matches strikes the mention of her name
light touches her arm: turn blind

your enemy (who the story tries to catch out)
to destroy this peace, to poison, to control this experience

religion wears that shoed smile

...

stars start up angrily : gleaming : fixed
thunder it spat throughout the night

tea was drunk: there is innocence in refreshment

to join the cause we will go abroad,
(or frame the mission)
till the storm blows over, stand on this spot

jump from the wall : follow grown companions
the heart is inclined to jest
shake the obnoxious foundations of memory

where the sob ended, speech stole the liquid present
some entrance must haunt us:

who are the elated swelled others?

openness, comfort indeed
I have been afraid of the thing you said

...

after the accident, the brain's cheerful spell
consider the rotten scheme
(the author recognised the line's powerful agent)

I will forgive reason, this dishonourable act

but I cannot forget it (intend to observe it,
to stop the worn competition)
the head-wind spins, plays with human fortunes

mixes up the memories of old men
tradition: an old friend in close proximity
full, fake balance,
glad to believe there used to be ...

a glorious escape, the hammer voice strikes ////
what brings this crazy planet alive

... the cymbiform moon?

...

        will they map it again
            secret machines juggle numbers

notions: a thought, calculated to zero

    profit speaks with whipped earnestness
dog and fire recall present trouble

      to shake in the sun-flame furnace

     that never-never curve failed to rise
I think you must be inside it: rain bandied its weather
      launches a false report

        infernal : inferno, nobody has dressed down
   eager his panache made others squeal

         rise immediately, anticipate and ask
    what is driving you (pause) speak

    destruction one-eyed; inclement
nothing rash in the diamond whisper
   quiet: let moist skies overflow; but no need to lecture

      ...

the dog sprang up to fetch,
arm struck out to overthrow a commanding gesture
startling rapidity of strange incidents

knit this notion, be aware of promises
instinctively distrust butyric words

the stealthily indignation galvanised opinion

...

figures bump, balance an attitude of indexes
an even hand is a smothered tone

wild on any terms observe this thread
a tour de force, as I listen at the window
turn for one last glimpse

the echo hears nothing
let the tall poppy pass

returning to the outer oval
witness the tortured treetops; reception casts thought

aligning and moving gracefully
pass a hat, straighten that flower

surmise a great controversy:
whose image dwells in the memory of motion?

insight some type of great petite idea
history represents an amiable allotment

objects always robust, admired and agreeable
the inevitable lot of humanity
snatch to fit the slave of routine

organisation sowed the restless ant colony

...

birds position poles
present what is elevated : frenetic : still

what is to be told: mind is made up to take flight

what if your command will burst-forth, if you give nothing
beyond the eye's glittering gateway

reflection flees the moment of arrival

blazing across the prairie, the fire horse traveller
to reflect, embrace the flood that time consumes

where the roof rises, boats sail
parturient hope subtracts importance

you look for belief ... it's not so outrageous

I am a stranger
guests terminate this conversation

...

becoming scarlet
from the south the travelling carriage

x-rays are anterior
(to bear away the happy imagination)
embrace: you could scarcely describe this prison

a hunch, an encouraging age of corruption
I would faint plain sailing across the whispering universe

in a green tea valley, direction contiguous,
district of factories ... no space,
that unbalanced history

...

existence answerable
the morning was fine, rhyme clear, crystal-
line

a soft western breeze
the starting-post was about here
the attack: fork-lightning flashed ... scintillated

from every quarter of the frame, horizon bruised,
black thunder broke over earth

to have never felt it in its fullness
        now, never *hush … hush*, secrets
      nothing but idle gossip in your neck of the woods

…

     frantically trying to remember the message
in my last note, helplessness
       and what foregoes this conclusion

      a moment dries once more
         do negatives freeze light in motion?

it drives me up the wall … gently, it's dangerous

not because this work was ill conceived: partly executed
    amid deciduous glades, amongst flowering galleries, curves often cir-

    cular …

        …

      cannot hold it closed, shut it within
this structure myself: shine-forth

      not yet a mine, a door silent
   strange … foreboding,
that it never transmutes a few general words of assent

necessary to grip an ugly vision: don't complicate
maybe it seems shallow to know what to do

colour flushed from face, comical and lost
tears stood in eyes, moment arranging belief

blink, and all that sleep : black : awake,

fragile figure; for, though
frozen, sound rightfully unearths
meaning, a watchful mind, mouth becomes page

...

I have endeavoured to picture something
to develop out loudly
portrait hanging, angled, re-

set, eye-levelled: see ... *mix-it-up*
(a pace or two towards the door)

flight is evident:
the suicidal career of what idea was then up-
tight, styled on this occasion, heart circulates

finding itself a home
desire, very likely tomorrow's attraction

point to a word : a figure ... high-
lights, characters of this familial history

...

why is the driving mind sitting still?
rested, posterity shatters the body

twilight an example of illumination
to cross the bridge I recognise nothing

flight made this place

the finely arched brow … a little elevated
grey dark rain; eyes fully opened

encouraging mental competitors

the frame has ridden underground
faithfully glanced at the brook

with the eye-lid folding in the midst
of this key, deep communion

sentiment kettles this light,
if only to enchain and frighten.

for Karl Stead (who excavated Dylan Thomas from the rubble)

A Strange Harvest ... A

SEISMIC SEA WAVE

a crescent phase : a compass rose

a trail of words in the heart of a plant

let's not mince words: pollen is plant sperm

tiny algae making sea water appear the colour of wine

vivid ....

sparks in golden lines joined at a star

even in death, dem bones are washed in red wine

proboscis monkeys pick their way through thickets of mangrove

2

INLAND [   ] Is-land: a detached home

incorrigible

herons plus one fish

equals

a flapping squabble over property rights

workers strip picture tubes from laughter

little girls from broken records

recycled domestic couples indulge in moments of twilight romance

cockpits enter a potentially deadly practice …

3

death is a little podcast …

ALLERGY GIRL

at night she dreams of spiders and insects

(hints of early human migration : hints of prehistoric failure)

borne to her burial, allergy girl speaks a condensed version:

Apsara

originally came to me in a flower

… Apsara, a celestial attendant … this mimetic spider un-

threading a world   dredged land reclaimed

where engineers nor mystics could stem the flow

where informal e-waste is processed

> *(spammed at a proximity to humans at .com)*

a strange harvest … a potential home for life

4

SIX MONTHS   alone in a cave

> *… who seeks to satisfy a spiritual hunger?*

… who will answer directly?

waiting for them to come out

> I used to be ashamed living here

(there is unbearable)   *but what else can I do?*

this house creates a strategy

forms   play out in the shadow of fiery peaks

same spot: sandy, barren, and bone-dry

creatures novel to science as they are to the eye

... scientists say it's inductive searching for signs

a bold new try for the top ...

a step into a world where gods displayed their powers

5

Å

            (above)

10,000 WINGS

            reflections flee one lightning bolt

rush of wings welcomes the dawn

            we who face death are becoming strangers

who stuck his head into a seal's breath?

            a question mark crosses the Arctic

                    ....?

.... FLOOD ....

        to ride inflate   (glimpse)

hundreds … of … thousands … of … bubbles

precious waters mirror a passing of canyons

a magical city

more a dormitory town now

bowls regularly played in parks

two local bands: one the Salvation Army

6

a mushroom cloud of stone erupts

… morals become personal   *and he is born*

JOHN DIAMOND

a blind scholar

a well-known traveller

best known for promoting the use of the umbrella

he pretends to his son

insights are undeniably interesting

(practical skills with some formal learning)

living a forlorn existence

an expert trainer of acrobatic fleas

    he throws missiles and horse-chesnuts

lined up on three sides of a square we continue in that role today

7

    GROUND ZERO

: the floor …

    see what happens after creating art

from accidents and vandalism … show me a face worthy of love

stencils of hands – mysterious ions, or shamanistic rituals …

    powers for a better life

my aim is to improve this situation safeguard the local environment

    there is a string down the middle a loop at the base

    ………. *distance unwinding* …

a train running eastwards: four trains in each direction

yesteryear the omnibus carried the byway

time rents a moving truck

on the horizon   a cowboy props up his horse.

The Tombstone Epitaph

I

a cowboy on his horse props up the horizon …

fourteen hundred dollars and a faro layout were found in his room

II

the horizon   on his horse a cowboy propped up

The Epitaph gives an account of the killing (*The Tucson Daily Citizen* indorses the news) while no particulars are published the whole story is too well known to require repetition

III

propped up on the horizon   a cowboy   his horse

… headed for Albuquerque   being pursued by an Arizona posse two desperadoes and five of their confederates arrive on the Atlantic & Pacific Express, the party are outlaws and fugitives from justice, without doubt the most desperate men now at large

IV

his horse on the horizon   a cowboy pops up

(while in town) the party's presence is withheld by local papers   described briefly in a letter: the complete text of the letter decontextualised … gamblers and saloon men are running things

… there is a general feud in and about Tombstone a continuous war between the two factions

V

props   up on the horizon   a cowboy   his horse

Virgil is the city marshal of Tombstone he holds the peace and quiet in the hollow of his hand … wounded   he is now at his home in San Bernardino

VI

his horse up on a horizon   the cowboy stops

hardly a day in which a cocked revolver had not been levelled at someone (seven dead cowboys bearing witness to the accuracy of their aim) two lives taken for each one lost

VII

the cowboy stops his horse upon a horizon

they have become a terror to the entire country, telegraphs from Tombstone … *party departs leaving earlier than expected after an argument …*

VIII

on a horizon his horse   up pops the cowboy

(it appears that in Tombstone a general feeling of regret was still very much alive: the quarrel referred to would be the same one mentioned in the letter)

IX

props   the cowboy   his horizon upon a horse

inferentially words cannot express the regret felt – the unhappy result
of triggernometry – the intended reparation will have to be deferred to a
singular type of desperado, if a desperado at all

X

a horse upon his horizon   a cowboy stops

your true fighting man talks very little of his exploits, removed from the
scene rioters and frontiersman in general they were men whose deeds
became known among the rounders

XI

a cowboy stops his horizon up on the horse

they left Arizona and came to Albuquerque (seven in all) they would not
give themselves up, knowledge of their whereabouts would bring a posse
of cowboy avengers down upon them

XII

on the horse a cowboy props up his horizon

(the party disbanded) Tombstone supplied a posse of man-hunters who it
appears this morning at last found their prey . . .

XIII

his horizon cropped   the cowboy   horse   (once) upon a ...

P.S. Virgil Earp was not among the group that made its way to Albuquerque. The latest news from the quondam Albuquerqueans, the Earp crowd, is that Wyatt, Warren and Virgil Earp are in San Francisco, engaged in dealing faro. Texas Jack is in Colorado, Doc Holliday in Leadville, McMasters and Johnson in Mexico, and Tipton in the Gunnison country.

Unearthed Vestiges

Flashlight on a broken column
    six linked inscriptions

        unearthed vestiges
youthful vigour, rickshaws haul-

          ing yesterday's diffusion

     the rhythms of conversation
        familiar hills : topography …

        worn apart by rapid repetition

     wheels pulling outer sparks in-
  wards …
        to be turned about completely

having uncovered a serious flaw
    building sentences: set of fields woven together … across : cross-
        stitched, a little bit tighter around outskirts
connecting a small revolutionary component
      mark it   strengthen it (in other regions)
       stick it:
           interplay between
               icono-
               stases

        ————————

   surface, fresh battle grounds mix
shell-game urgency

just allow them to fidget

occidental disturbances will affect sustainability
wayward we expect this to be a decisive test

                    a sizeable difference in arrival times
              illusions creating a sacred place

          craters … clusters, circling further out
    bottom-line excavations

          _____

              sectionals
          a tiny fraction of a second

              tell-tale footprints : time's unseen ghosts
                        this year will plug generalities
          sensitive enough
    to produce a flash of light … élan

          what will slip through unseen …?

          constellation as gear to the swarm
    we need both approaches: this is not the same story

       surveying the whole sky once every few days
              twice building an unprecedented picture of perspective

              reverence, I think … heightened readings
          there could be a sting in this tale,
                    myriad faint, or invisible celestial circuitry.

She is Sparrow-like and Fierce

I'll tie myself to her voice

scene pulled from frame to frayed edge
      knot-to-knot ... to pull backwards that tapestry of dress

          (yes, the pattern returns triumphant)
            crux of the matter, to go on ... wistfully

               could not she?

            of course life-lines feeding the concrete

          clear-cut she is sparrow-like and fierce,
      thin ... angular, with the hollow-eyed look

     she could reach people with her mimicry
        a little melancholic roust

an elegiac circus   and under this whirling
     her manic joy ... streaming in and out-of-breath.

       for my mother, a whirling dervish on her 60th birthday

My leaves have drifted from me. All. But one clings still. I'll bear it on me. To remind me of. Lff! So soft this morning, ours. Yes. Carry me along, taddy, like you done through the toy fair!

— JAMES JOYCE, *FINNEGANS WAKE*

Six Reels of Joy

... as shadow   a light   and body

in the present tense ... a quint-
essence

a paly of six argent and azure
a cinquefoil gules in the centre of a sun

(names displaced by light
are dark but not lost ...

) ... Miss Lucia

2

in my headiness

light against the Earth's axial tilt
against the axes of both bodies
(glass) bodies
of alphabetical bones

one
by one, scattered frames ... the low off-
shore islands ... over-
lapping scraps of the water's reflection

3

re-verse soundings   :

                    mirror   images
          of mother   father
                da & ma

the nature of divination

                between saint and certitude
          to within a second . . . scenarios

like the sunrise centred and sunset rendered

                (or vice versa)

4

Zeroth————Zohar————Zygote
          tracking … *shadow this, take and come up*

                shadow, come to the present … the sur-
face … the Lion————the Light————the Luminous

5

August

heart
head
helix

DNA   X
tracing

Y

(past Adam's Peak and Zion Track, from swerve of-shore to bend of-bay
            to Z of-land … Zzzzzzz … sunrise … a-

wake, Lucia *re-*
sprung in us by carnal equinox) A – Z

6

:   dialectical

              the pull and push

        part and parcel … the abstract un-

folding   lucid

the birth, the human, the light

THE HUMAN-LIGHT

flowing out and *through us*
this
is flesh

daughter

a likeness   (chorus)
of that   unknown   rushing

(through
us))))))))))))))))))

the pulse   trace
  elements

                                arc-
                      ing
            through
            us

    luna ... (lady)   *leo (baby) ...*
lupus (gypsy) ... lux-

        Lucia.

for my daughter

Notes

The epigraph on the dedication page is from Samuel Beckett, *Worstward Ho* (London: John Calder, 1983), p. 13.

'Halcyon Ghosts' builds its form from Harvey Benge's bookwork *Birds*. The photographs were taken from the deck of a Devonport ferry as it headed into Auckland Harbour on the afternoon of Thursday, 15 July 2010. The first epigraph is from Michael Palmer's *Thread* (New York: New Directions, 2011), p. 90; many thanks to Michael Palmer for permission to use this text.

The second epigraph is from John Cage, 'Lecture on Commitment' (1961), in *A Year from Monday* (Middletown, CT: Wesleyan University Press, 1967), p. 119.

'Erasure' is dedicated to Don Binney (1940–2012), an artist and conservationist best known for his paintings of birds. Geoff Moon (1915–2009), naturalist and exceptional bird photographer, is also an inspiration for this piece.

'Flushed from a Tidal Retreat' has its origins in the oldest unequivocal document of origami, a short poem composed by Ihara Saikaku in 1680. It is dedicated to my father, Colin John Sampson (1944–2014).

'All the Everlasting Cataracts' is a line from Keats's 'Hyperion' (1819).

'I Spilled My Story' was part of the collaborative exhibition *You Have Changed Me Already* (with artist Peter Madden) at the Ivan Anthony Gallery, March 2012, Auckland.

'Broken Architecture' is dedicated to poet C. K. Stead. After reading 'Broken Architecture' Karl replied in kind, with the poem 'Back then (but briefly)' (*The Yellow Buoy*, Auckland University Press, 2013, p. 69), which he says 'strangely turned out to be "about" visiting the grave of Dylan Thomas in 1957'.

'The Tombstone Epitaph' uses excerpts from articles and newspaper clippings collected at BlongerBros.com. The title is taken from the

Arizona-based monthly publication (est. 1880) – the oldest continually running newspaper in Arizona.

Halcyon Ghosts recycles source material from writers: Rae Armantrout, Samuel Beckett, John Cage, Peter Cole, John Donne, T. S. Eliot, Barbara Guest, James Joyce, John Keats, Michael Palmer, Gustaf Sobin, Wallace Stevens, Dylan Thomas and Louis Zukofsky.

For more information on the author and associated collaborations, please visit: www.samsampson.co.nz

•

Many of these poems appeared, sometimes in a slightly different form, in: *Best New Zealand Poems 2012, Cordite Poetry Review, JAAM, Turbine* and *Shearsman Magazine.*

Broken Architecture / Salt Away (2010), with Andrew Grace, a selection of poems, was published as part of the Duets chapbook series, which pairs poets from New Zealand and the United States.

… exclusivity dwells in habitat (FAQEDITIONS: 2012) was published as a collaborative bookwork with photographer Harvey Benge.

Thanks to the team at Auckland University Press, especially; Anna Hodge, Katrina Duncan, Sam Elworthy and Christine O'Brien who have been a pleasure to work with.

And love as always to Jacinda, whose extraordinary support made this book possible; and Lucia, our daughter, who twists and turns throughout this collection … *of time past and time future …*

Sam Sampson was born in Auckland, New Zealand, and grew up in Titirangi. His poetry has been widely published in journals and chapbooks, and his first collection with Auckland University Press, *Everything Talks*, won the NZSA Jessie Mackay Best First Book Award for Poetry at the 2009 book awards.